DYING IN A MOTHER TONGUE

EMERGING VOICES FROM THE MIDDLE EAST

Series Editor
Dena Afrasiabi

Other titles in the series include *Using Life* and *Limbo Beirut*

DYING IN A MOTHER TONGUE

ROJA CHAMANKAR

Translated by *Blake Atwood*

CENTER FOR MIDDLE EASTERN STUDIES
The University of Texas at Austin

Library of Congress Control Number: 2018956068
ISBN: 978-1477317808

Translated from Roja Chamankar *Mordan Be Zaban-e Madari* 2nd Edition (Tehran: Cheshmeh, 2012)

Cover illustration by Kai Tran
Book and cover designs by Allen Griffith of Eye 4 Design

CONTENTS

Contents

TRANSLATOR'S NOTE

I read Persian poetry in its original language for the first time as an undergraduate at the University of Virginia. I was a young student of the Persian language, and my mentor entrusted me with a photocopied stack of pages containing several poems by Forugh Farrokhzad in their original Persian. It seemed like a big responsibility for a nineteen year-old from a small town in the mountains of Virginia. The experience, though, was exhilarating, as shapes gave way to words and to images and sounds that I never imagined possible. Since that first memorable encounter, Persian poetry has been a regular presence in my life, consistently reminding me of the boundless potential of the Persian language: its music, its wits and charms, its ambiguity in some moments and unsparing directness in others. As more of my academic life centered on Persian, the language became a second home for me, with poetry as the concrete foundation. Despite this intimate relationship, whenever someone asked me to recommend my favorite poem, I never felt sure enough in my answer; that is, until I read "The Start," the first poem in *Dying in a Mother Tongue* by Roja Chamankar. Suddenly and unexpectedly, I had a favorite Persian poem.

Before reading *Dying in a Mother Tongue*, I had never been moved to translate poetry. As much as I enjoyed existing between English and Persian, part of the pleasure lay in selfishly keeping them separate. With *Dying in a Mother Tongue*, however, I felt compelled to explore what it would mean to hunt for Persian in a forest of English: to render words, images, and entire worlds into a new language for a whole new readership. I was driven by my belief that these are poems too spectacular to be cradled in a single language, that this poet's voice deserves to be heard echoing through many places.

It is impossible to even broach the topic of women's poetry in Iran without mentioning Forugh Farrokhzad (1935-1967), a poet who not only helped establish a feminine voice in modern Persian poetry but who also has achieved cult-like status in Iran, inspiring subsequent generations of readers and writers. Farrokhzad's poetry—which deals with issues of women's sexuality alongside of questions of gender, artistry, death, and decay—is not always easily accessible in Iran, and it is certainly not taught in schools or universities. Nevertheless, since Farrokhzad's untimely death at age 32, readers have found their way to her poetry like a beacon in the night, and it continues to find resonance in the lives and work of those women poets who have been writing in the years since. Early pioneers of women's poetry in Iran, like Farrokhzad, Parvin E'tesami (1907-1941), and Tahereh Qorrat al-'Ayn (1817-1852), carried the incredible burden of having to represent all women for all people. Even a tireless champion like Farrokhzad often reflected on her sense of defeat under the weight of this responsibility; the title of her last collection of poetry, *Let Us Believe in the Beginning of the Cold Season*, published posthumously in 1974, captures her frustrations and disappointments.

Chamankar and her contemporaries, however, have the benefit of numbers. Because there are now many successful women poets—and deservedly so—no one poet is responsible for representing all their concerns. As a result, we see this generation of women poets experimenting with themes, styles, images, and language that are entirely new to Persian poetry. While the experience of being a woman certainly undergirds Chamankar's work and that of her peers, readers no longer expect to find the totality of a woman's experience in a single collection of poetry. Roja Chamankar is proudly a woman poet, but her work does not need to be women's poetry. Chamankar's poetry is confident in its female voice but successful because of her musings on sensuality, insights into human relations, colorful images of Iran's southern landscape, and masterful control of the Persian language.

Even within the robust and growing tradition of contemporary Persian poetry, Roja Chamankar has distinguished herself among the best. She was born in 1981 in Borazjan, a small city in the southeast province of Bushehr, Iran. Two formative experiences shaped her childhood: proximity to the sea and the experience of war. Bushehr is a tropical, coastal province of palm trees and seashores. But during the eight-year war between Iran and Iraq (1980-1988), it was also on the frontlines due to its strategic location on the Persian Gulf. The last five poems of *Dying in a Mother Tongue* are the most autobiographical in the collection, each taking the form of a letter to members of Chamankar's family. In these poems, we get a glimpse into the paradoxes of such a childhood: its intense beauty and its horrifying fear. In "For Bahar," a letter to her sister, for example, stars twinkling by the sea are juxtaposed with the pain of those "cloudy years." Chamankar's childhood was one that equipped her with a profound sense of injustice but also an appreciation for the beauty of Iran's southern landscape.

Despite the chaos of war, Chamankar's parents nurtured her love of art and literature from an early age. She lived in a house that cherished books and literature, and spent many hundreds of hours reading as a child. Chamankar began publishing her poetry in regional magazines and journals at age 11, and published her first collection of poetry, *You Left to Bring Me a Little Bit of the South*, in 2000 when she was 19. Since then, she has published nine collections of poems, selections of which have been translated into French. Her collections of poetry have garnered numerous awards, including the Parvin E'tesami Prize in Iran and the prestigious Nikos Gatsos Prize in France. In addition to her poetry,

x Chamankar has published three children's books (co-authored with her father) and numerous translations of French poetry into Persian. Also accomplished in cinema and theater, she has made two short films, produced documentaries for the BBC, and written film scripts and plays.

****

Two opposing forces shape *Dying In A Mother Tongue*: intimacy and disillusionment. And it is here that readers familiar with Forugh Farrokhzad's poetry might find similarities between these two important poets. On the one hand, many of the images and scenes in *Dying in a Mother Tongue* are intimate. They are moments shared by lovers, meaningful glances between strangers, the life and death of family, and a sharp focus on marginal figures. But it isn't just the closeness between people in the poems that make the collection intimate. It is also the poet's point of address: the first-person voice, the frequent use of the informal second-person, and the invitation to participate in the sometimes mundane and sometimes spectacular moments that the poems narrate. To read *Dying in a Mother Tongue* is to experience intimacy in every manner and meaning of the word. On the other hand, the poems in this collection are marked by disappointment and loss. Death, separation, political disillusionment, and injustice are themes that run throughout the collection, punctuating and sometimes puncturing the closeness we feel to the poet and her subjects.

Capturing both intimacy and disillusionment in a single, brief collection of poetry is no small task. Chamankar achieves this feat by activating a surrealist mode that operates in the grey space between real and imaginary. A poem like "The Smokey Taste of Water" epitomizes Chamankar's surreal imagery. The poem references actual, everyday places like the Shahid Dastgerdi Overpass in Tehran, but just a stanza later the poet becomes a darkroom spewing red light like blood. Similarly, the evocative poem "The Seaweed's

Magic" imagines the underwater desires of algae as they dance and tangle in the crosscurrent. For over a millennium, Persian poets have addressed themes of intimacy and disillusionment through carefully coded images: the moth and the flame, the rose and the nightingale, wine, intoxication, and beauty marks. With images like hanging eye sockets ("Until Those Ripe Words Made Me Bitter"), shitty skies ("The Smokey Taste of Water"), and dried-out butterflies, ("Bits and Pieces of Me"), these poems explode the motifs of classical Persian poetry. *Dying in a Mother Tongue* demands that ambiguity and ambivalence, mainstays of Persian poetic tradition, be updated to account for the injustices of our contemporary world and to resonate with the lives of readers today.

The title *Dying in a Mother Tongue* captures the mood of the collection, both the disillusionment that it describes and the intimacy it aspires to. The act of dying is juxtaposed with the figure of the mother and one's native language—both sites of sensuality. At the same time, the title evokes the life cycle: birth and death and how they come full circle. With this in mind, it is not surprising that Chamankar describes this collection to me as grounded in the experience of adulthood. Some context is helpful here. Chamankar wrote this collection between 2008 and 2009, and it was published in 2010. Written as she prepared to leave Iran for France, *Dying in a Mother Tongue* anticipates the experience of parting; its language longs for reconnection and seeks out closeness even before the trauma of separation. At the same time, the collection reflects on Iran in the second half of the first decade of the 21st century, as the country's economy worsened and its ties to the outside world became more precarious. The poems in *Dying in a Mother Tongue* capture these emotions by activating imagery from traditional folktales and mythology: dungeons, Egyptian handmaids, magical seaweed, and jinns.

At the same time, Chamankar evokes this particular moment in her life by bringing the lush southern landscape of her hometown Bushehr to the hard, unforgiving capital city of Tehran. She sets up this tension in the first line of the collection's first poem, "The Start," as she writes, "When I speak of Tehran, I end up at the sea." This statement haunts the rest of the collection, as the reader finds herself transported again and again from subway stations and busy intersections to seashores and palm groves. The southern landscape is one of the hallmarks of Chamankar's poetry. She is part of a long tradition of women poets in Iran, many of whom also narrate small moments and domestic, urban spaces. And yet Chamankar is unique among Persian poets in the vastness of her imagery, a mark of the diversity of Iran and its geography. It is a country of cement and skyscrapers, mountains and deserts, and forests and shorelines. In *Dying in a Mother Tongue*, each of these landscapes evokes a different sense of intimacy or disillusionment.

****

Roja Chamankar gave me a copy of *Dying in a Mother Tongue* when we first met in Tehran in the spring of 2016. For months after, I wore down the pages of that copy, reading poem after poem in silence or in the company of my own voice. Later, I would have the opportunity to hear Chamankar recite her poetry in public, in places like the deserts of Yazd and the small feminist bookshops of Austin, Texas. No other experience shaped my approach to translating her work more than these public readings. As I followed her from venue to venue, I watched each time as Chamankar commanded the room. Empty handed, without a single note, she performed her poems, and even though the mostly English-speaking audiences couldn't understand her words, they knew their grandeur. A witness to these sincere moments of mutual understanding, I felt confident in my decision to translate her poetry but, more importantly, I realized that these translations would need to be read aloud as companions to her recitations. As she and I reviewed my renditions throughout the translation process, I found myself often saying, "Now listen to this." Replicating the sonic textures of her Persian became a priority.

It is easy to measure a translation by its losses, and there are, of xiii course, many losses in the translations that follow. Chamankar's Persian celebrates doing a lot with very little. It plays with the fact that Persian depends on compound structures that group and regroup simple words to create entirely new meanings. In Persian, for example, a verb that literally translates as "to give from the hand" (*az dast dādan*) actually means to lose something. The poems in *Dying in a Mother Tongue* draw our attention to the density of Persian—a density that most speakers are not even aware of. Naturally, it was impossible to capture the linguistic playfulness of these poems; each instance would have required an entire language lesson. To belabor each of these moments would have meant moving further and further away from my goal of rendering these poems into readable English that could supplement Chamankar's recitations while also standing on their own. I never wanted these poems to be strictly academic translations that accomplish more as explications than they do as poetry.

In the translations, I acknowledge some of these moments of playfulness by using similar word play in English or by adjusting the poetry's tempo in order to approximate the repetition of words in the compound structures in the original Persian. Rather than mourn these losses, they are instead opportunities to celebrate the sophistication of the poems. Translations are always imperfect and incomplete. The tension between their successes and failures creates openings for reflection on the role of translation in the first place. The failures are an invitation to the reader to pause, to think, and to engage further, but so too are the successes.

The compound structures that the poems in *Dying in a Mother Tongue* love to pull apart often draw our attention to the body. In Persian, words like head, hand, and foot get coupled and reconfigured to make some of the most basic meanings in everyday life. In the example above, for instance, "to give from the hand" actually means to "lose." *Hampā*, which literally means "someone who shares a foot," actually means companion ("Behind the Curtain"). By drawing our attention to the body parts that underpin so much meaning in Persian, Chamankar adds to the intimacy that structures the xiv collection as a whole. Indeed, the poems in *Dying in a Mother Tongue* narrate small moments and describe small images made big through incredible language. It was precisely this quality that made translating her work sometimes effortless and at other times nearly impossible. While acknowledging the playfulness of her language or rendering the simplicity of her verse were sometimes challenging in English, the translatability of her images will mean that the poems still resonate with English-speaking readers. The poem "Close-up," for example, begins with the line "It happens in a closed frame," which immediately establishes the tight focus of Chamankar's poetic lens. It continues by likening the touch of love making to the sensuality of preparing food. The cramped space of a small urban apartment—a living arrangement that most readers can appreciate—intensifies the intimacy of the speaker's gaze. With a title like "Close-up," such a poem demonstrates how Chamankar's training as a filmmaker has shaped her poetry. The images she constructs are carefully framed. Sometimes beautiful, nearly always haunting, they resonate in any language.

Readers hoping to find familiar tropes of oppressed women or an exotic Iran might be disappointed when they read this collection. The poems in *Dying in a Mother Tongue* offer so much more than the tired representation of Iran that has become common in English publications. These poems are portraits of everyday life in Iran at a time when economic and political frustrations ran high; they are masterful feats because they accomplish so much while also saying so little. Too often the act of reading a translation takes on an almost ethnographic quality. We are confronted with a text polished in one language but with the full knowledge that it was born in another. This sets us on a mission to pin down the scraps of authenticity, to locate the original after it has been stripped of its mother tongue. My hope is that the translations in the volume that follows are not the death of these poems but rather a rebirth that will inspire new readers, new readings, new meanings, and even new translations.

DYING IN A MOTHER TONGUE

THE START

When I speak of Tehran, I end up at the sea
when I speak of myself or of you,
when I speak of the sky, I end up at the sea.
When I distance myself from it, forgetting,
starting fresh, I end up back at the sea.

Where is the leak in this sea
as all of my relationships turn tender?
Drenched, they end up at the sea.

THE KNOT

I stare at my fists
and think of my heart
and the knot that's always
in my throat torments me.
For every heartbeat,
I've flogged myself with words
in the kitchen, in your small bedroom
on the surface of your wooden table
at the very end of your hidden sanctuary.

I look at my long fingernails
and the scratchmarks that were
always in my veins torment me.
Like a mother feeding her chicks
you place pain in my mouth
fire in my stomach
and then you leave.

I think of the size of my heart
and untangle the knot to wave goodbye.
How awful that a train
is the most poetic mode of transportation.

GREEN LIGHT

Just like that, you scatter
into someone's crowded life
with vacant eyes
purple
   green
      blue
and just like that you fall asleep
on all of his favorite colors
cross over his yellow shirt
smash the red light
and drink up its blood
without hearing the cars behind you
honking their horns.

Just like that, you rip the moon
from the sky's throat
and lay it flat in the middle of the crossroads
scatter dirt over its beauty
and you scatter

just like that
and cars are honking
and you stare into her eyes
just like that
and you throw back your drink
in a cozy corner of chaos
and you don't hear that behind you . . .
and you don't see that the crossroad
has only one road
that leads to the moon's artificial light.

INVITATION

All roads are closed to me
I've climbed up your eyelashes
don't shut your eyes.

THE SMOKEY TASTE OF WATER

You know that this moon
clashes with the city's shitty skies
that this tree who clings to our
wall with a thousand hands,
clashes with the city's smoky color,
that the fortuneteller
perched tiny on the Shahid Dastgerdi Overpass,
clashes with the city's small desires.

I'm like a darkroom now,
blood-red light spewing
from my head
and you know
that this lost blood will
never come back.

Quiet, black gloves
make their way,
easy lies

make their way,
mass shootings
lost lands
knife handles
all make their way to us.
They let you enjoy your food today,
and tomorrow
split you in half.

You know how bitter
the water tastes

UNTIL THOSE RIPE WORDS MADE ME BITTER

They blinked, and the wind
swirled in their hanging sockets.
They blinked, and blood
swirled in their hanging sockets.
They blinked, and pain
swirled in their hanging sockets.
These stones
with amputated thumbs
they blinked, and your voice
swirled in their hanging sockets

Blood came from within
a well, an angel, and a demon, too.
I let them make me bitter
along the wind's defiant path.
I kissed your bones and your lips with my poetry
I let them ripen
turn seven years-old,
I let them make me bitter.

I scattered your voice
onto the wind's defiant path
hung it on the clothesline
for the sparrows,
placed it diagonally in the sun's vertical rays.
I let myself sit inside your laughter
until it made me bitter,
until the sun shining in my eyes,
my hair growing long
hallowing out and hanging,
your laughter blowing through my curls
made me bitter.
Your hands ripened
and your lips did too
until those ripe words made me bitter.
These stones,
with cut thumbs
and veins made of your cries,
your laughter, your voice

they gashed open, and blood
swirled in their hanging sockets.
I should have woken up.
The god of Babel,
The god of deep wells
bitter wine
dream towers,
the god of farewells
on that night when it snowed.

STAND CLEAR

I'm detached from myself
from your voice
from my bond with the sparrows
and the moon
who drags the sky down to the earth.
I can't connect
to the crowded station
smashed lips
monochrome clothes
bells and buzzers.

I can't connect
to this stretched-out space
the screaming skulls
the strange, compact shapes.
The shape of looking into someone else's eyes
of touching someone else's hand,
a hand that rejects while saving you,
a hand that saves while rejecting you.

Such is love:
like a gash
its mouth opens up
and its two heads never meet
Stand clear of the closing doors.

Dark cars
dark chocolates
undergarments
saleswomen
a toxic voice
Stand clear of the train doors
and the door
turns on the tip of my high heels.

CLOSE-UP

It happens inside a closed frame
with the smell of garlic, herbs, and onions
garnish for that moment in the kitchen.
When I close my eyes,
you appear from the denial of those first words
from the denial of water and fire and oak trees
and the burnt fruits under my dress.
A little bit of flour
holds it all together.
It happens inside a closed frame
in steam rising from the water
pepper and spices on my lips
tamarind
the sound of bangles
the knife's sharp tip on the slippery body of a fish
the murmur of two shadows on the flimsy cabinet
the lights go out
the sound goes out.
It's nothing.

The light bulbs always short circuit
in a building with four apartments and four stories
on the fourth floor
with no parking or storage.
Inside a closed frame
in black and white
it happens.

Under a faint flame
I was tender to the touch.

WHEN THE WEATHER CHANGES

One long scream shoots out of me
and my veins split open.
You're not here
and now the procession moves into the room
over a shower of ants.

All my loving
leads nowhere but to a dusty alley,
to someone's lips
pressed against mine.

We've wrecked the careful arrangement
of this room with ants,
fat, black ants
barely any blood under their skin.
You left with a flute of sand
which I put under your skin
in place of my own instrument.

Under all of your excuses
under the helpless grains of sand settled in the room
I installed
a full-length mirror made of me.
You can break inside of me and each time
only see blood from the pain of denial.

The sea
has leaked into my room.
The ants need CPR.
They should learn to die less.
They are my only childhood hobby.
When the weather changes
I will tell the sea
to carry me away
to a dusty alley.

You were supposed to look out for me.

FINISH ME

Take aim
at the connected pieces
and scatter toward me on the helix of night
Everything ends up at its own beginning
from its own end
even if you turn your back on the scraps of my heart
even if I return from disaster
and the miracle does not sink into the earth
and no one gazes at the dark-colored
residue on the edges of pain.

Even if holy, intoxicated blood
splatters on the helix of night
even if the most hidden
corners of the earth tremble
even if all these pieces are the disjointed
parts of my unending dreams

even if I am the most inconsequential published disaster
in the darkest cavern of the earth
everything ends up at its own beginning
from its own end
even if the beginning
is only meant for arriving
at the end.

Finish me
take the fragrant oil from my body
pour syrup on my quiet waist
I am stuck to the ending
I am frozen.
Take aim
at my heart's cut pieces
its name
its nostalgia

I am stuck to the ending
and what remains of me protects
the gates of the sea
even if the sea
is not a clear path
to salvation.

I'LL PERISH

Gypsy!
This world was not my world
this voice was not my voice
your music silenced, my ears filled.
Outside this room, everything is for sale:
worn-out hearts
worn-out love
repetitive words
the futility of things
the blood of rubbish
the stuff of life is for sale.
Gypsy!
Wrap yourself around me like a never-ending piece of rhubarb
let's leave eternity for those who are afraid
whose laughter is an injection

whose beauty is an injection
and their blood, too

Strum my vein's copper strings
for your tears were salty
the path to my sea so far
one day I'll charge
towards harder times
and I'll perish, Gypsy
among the people's anguish
I'll plant myself in the earth
the orange tree, the date tree, and those other kinds, too
will bear fruit in me.
And this, my dark gypsy,
is how I deliver news of you

to a bright morning
a lush tree
a giving sun

After I'm gone,
be kind to this mummified moment
tuck away the secrets of this room
from the customers' eyes.

THE SIGN

Yellow irises
An old leather suitcase
And a poem stuck in my throat
When you're next to me,
My moon doesn't swing from sky to sky!

THE SANCTUARY

With a tiny torch I arrived to your welcome
with the sound of footsteps on snow
a damp dungeon and
a mass of wide-open black mouths.
I hung netting on the windows
for fear that the faceless moon
would reach my narrow spaces.
I pulled my cashmere scarf from the sky
down to the earth

the window
destroyed by stones
suffered a great defeat
at the hands of the room
I stretched myself
from sky to earth
by clinging to the moon
I looked out in the distance
and you greeted me.

Now
on the midnight of my winter
tell the snow to fall silently
with nothing but this pillaged land
and the teacup I haven't washed
so that you will always be by my side.

THE SEAWEED'S MAGIC

On tree trunks
earth, rocks, and snow
Haliptus!
Seaweed sighs
under sweet and salty waters
enchanting
swallowing the world
green figures
a terrifying blast.
Green
no longer
a blend of my blue gulf and your yellow sun.
Seaweed doesn't know
much about colors
about screams
that require courage
I don't want to explode

into the waters' enormous disgrace
To spill onto rocks and stems and snow
Seaweed sighs
under sweet and salty waters.

I am pregnant with curses
pollution and pain.
Pull me in
pour into my gulf!
Drag me out of my body's eternal shaking.
Haliptus!
Hidden from the seaweed, your sin
trickles onto my skin.
growing
infecting my blood
My blood runs to the earth
while my heart goes to the water.

Slide your hand over
the piano of my back
tip-tap
notes on the hard black-and-white shells
Let me become possessed
on the flanks of your voice
the madness of your voice
the seaweed's celebration interrupted
Haliptus!
Seaweed
grows in the harsh light
make me dark instead
among the impossible textures of your body
I don't want to glide on the rocks, the stems, and the snow
seaweed sighs
under sweet and salty waters.

Slime woven to the mouths of fish
grass-green fish
inhaling at the corners of this blast.
Seaweed is born
for tiny chunks of life
for new forms of war
    war
       war
           until whatever victory

Seaweed,
born from the touch
of a few symmetrical shapes
a few asymmetrical figures
of death's broken ribs.
Clinging to rocks
hanging on stems and snow
seaweed sighing
under sweet and salty waters.

I am hooked
they scratch at me
pulling me to my death, to their harsh light
if I am dark, hidden from the seaweed . . .
if I, hidden from the seaweed . . .
am a fine place for your sin to drip
to swell
a refuge for the child of your sin
if I, hidden from the seaweed . . .
fell in love with you
so be it.

ON THE EDGE

Let's leave
this moldy painting
through the dungeon's
drunken ceiling.
Let's leave these dark, splattered colors
on the four directions of this well.

The narrow alley
Zipporah's door was wooden
My nights were lost
and I was left alone, an orange doll
with two chunky eyes in hand.

Rectangular bubbles float up
and triangles
have sharp angles
that wear down the earth
and decapitate the sea.

And love
in the truest sense of the word:
love on the edge
love with fear
disastrous, all-powerful
love in dependence and devotion.
Where in this circle has love cowered?
Let's go.
Let's leave this dungeon.
Our love
for blades of grass
is more intense.
Don't love me anymore!

YOU HAVE REMAINED IN MY HEART LIKE A LETTER

The words appear in your absence
They scatter all over my destruction
cling to my life like pain.
You have stayed in my heart like a letter
stuck to the month of August
and to my death
and to your burgundy shirt
that covers up my veins.

The words come in your absence
from *you got used to losing me*
to *I kiss you from afar.*
Dying away from you wasn't easy.

If I come back to you, I will turn into a pillar of salt
and if I come back to myself, an Egyptian handmaid.

Next to your loving,
your absence scatters on my destruction
gets stuck to my life.

Pull me away from words
from your shirt
from the ruins of a pillar in Borazjan

BITS AND PIECES OF ME

They stick to my half-open mouth
forty dried-up butterflies.
They stick to bits and pieces of me
and no matter how many times I slide over myself
your blood doesn't flow into my body.

It ruptures my dreams
that burning needle of snow
an ulcer growing inside of me
widening up to my half-opened mouth
it can't become part of me.
It postpones my life.

Forty nights pass
forty seashells
lift the four corners of the sea
my veins are
always empty, full, empty.

I fill with a terrible pain
and faraway voices
grandmother's tales
I saw them with my own eyes
Shāhlān
Dālān
the yellow barberries of Ālān
jinns pour into her stories
steal my southern love
mate with bits and pieces of me,
melt, and refuse to sink into my body.
Then
forty nights pass
you return
and tell me about the melting snow
about the cranes' migration to the seashore.
I will become your snowman.

You will build me under the sun
with a dried-up butterfly on the corner of my lips
R-O-J-A
the scattered bits and pieces
are my own fault.

EVERYTHING A STORY

Aside from the safety of your temple,
which I stole from the seven kings,
stories are insignificant.
All that running is like carrying salt to the sea
all that moving up like squeezing water
all the seagulls grounded.
They find my footprint next to your lips.
Other than your gentle lips,
I would burn all this *once upon a time*
in a hot furnace
stuck to the walls of my childhood
to four o'clock in the morning, sticky, the power out
clinging to the strawmen in the alley,
who buried every everlasting thing
under the palm trees.
You
are my entire childhood.

I would burn everything in this story
except for your sand-colored arms
a safe shore
to save us from drowning
When I splay my hair on your face,
the sea begins to roar
whirling like the spokes of a wheel on a bike in Chitgar Park.
Spin me.
I love you in red satin.
Other than my love for you
I would burn everything in this story
except for the dance of light each time you blink
turning me into a beautiful black-and-white
photograph in your arms.
all of my loving
is the pulsing of your capillaries
in the small nights of the story . . .

Aside from your capillaries,
I would burn everything in this story.

The current of today's poetry
rushes from the veins of your temple.

FIREWORKS

It wasn't by accident
that you smelled my footprints underground.

My only escape route was a
stone tunnel that passed through your arms
mistaking my body for the gorges of Yasuj.

If only my eyes
were a sanctuary for your firecrackers
the comets would erupt from my screams
and speckle me onto the sky.

It wasn't an accident
that you threw a party
on the last Wednesday
of the year and ignited
red bushes on my skirt
and closed the valves
and I can barely breathe.

Sharp turns
your lips' lexical dangers
and wooden stems glide
over my silver skin.
You mistake me for
someone else
chew my roots
scatter me over the ground
by accident in the end
no one survives
the countdown
and later
you won't believe I'm not a star.
I'll become a lotus plant
and each day
you'll pass by
not recognizing me.

COPY

He just sat inside of me
searching me
searching my world
searching inside of me for the world.
He plucked a word from deep within my folds
and placed it on his temple
his brain decaying.
He sprinkled words
from his mouth onto my life.
The flimsy borders inside of me collapsed
my flimsy borders collapsed
I, a flimsy border, collapsed.

We were displaced.
I, a composite:
the world, searching, brains, life, borders, folds
decay, disintegration
and a second attempt at life
my second life!

Come breathe inside my death
we have been displaced
come breathe inside the world of my death
we have been displaced
come breathe the world within my death

There was always a word instead of me
that you could squander
on your temple
the laughter of your eyes

You, a copy from inside: words, waste, sawdust, death,
a vein through which you crossed my borders
a vein through which you crossed my borders!
You passed through my folds
you passed me by

ON A MIDNIGHT

I fell in love with you strangely.
You are my strangest lover
the most grotesque incident sketched
on the gulf at midnight
and I had been emptied of all signs of life

Deep within the scales of sea fortress walls
on those April nights
ghosts
appeal to the moon
gypsies
recite incantations and blow air.
You fan the eccentricity of a woman
with bangles that jingle
a knock-off necklace
from across the shore
and blood-red rubies
from a heart you shook in the wind.

You blink twice
and two dark tobacco leaves
appear in your eyes
turning my moments into smoke.
You ignite fire
on my bone-dry shoulders.
What have I done
with myself,
with my walls and bangles,
with this choked-up, gulf-less port?
Come away
far away
to the far-flung reaches of a body
dark and sandy.
Emptied of all signs of life
I blink twice
on a midnight
yearn once again

to fall in love with you, strangely
the most grotesque incident of
my April.

THE LAND IS LONELY

I'll be a coastal road
and you be the sea
my breath of fresh water!
Love me some other way.

BEHIND THE CURTAIN ·

My sweetheart!
The water was murky
and full of smoke
and no matter how many
different ways we
arranged the pieces
the ruins grew bigger
and more earthy
I cried out
la la la
to scamper the evil
away from you

Now
in the afternoons
how can I pass through
the ruptured streets

the wound-like trenches
of the water's injured body?
Dying in a mother tongue is hard
my darling
dying in a mother tongue . . .
Leave me alone
with my back to the ruins.
When my hands fall on the pieces
when curtains fall and
when trees fall on the way
I cry *la la la*
to make a whirlwind in the trenches

I wanted you to be
the right foot to my wandering
left foot in the afternoons.
There's nothing left to say

just a whoosh!
and this:
I wanted you to be
my heart.

A MUTUAL UNDERSTANDING

Somebody has meddled in my
poem for his own benefit
So I meddled in his life for my own benefit
Now for our mutual benefit
we avoid each other

FOR BAHAR

Turn off the lights
close your eyes
and listen to my voice through the seashell horn.
The sea is more beautiful
when stars twinkle next to dirty streams
and darkness always comes to the earth from the sky
like the black alley of those "cloudy years," and the pain that pushed
our homeland's brain to insanity
shaking from the cold in the heat of 50 degrees
and we
would not kneel
before the Strait of Bulhayat
or sour plums
bitter plums
frightened, red plums
dirty men, dirty women, and dirty streams
a sky that was blue in a story world
but not in my childhood.

The sea is more beautiful
when you laugh and water
fills the dimples in your cheeks.

Now go
pick up the seashell
and hide the sound inside.

FOR AMAJ

Turn off the lights
close your eyes
and listen to my voice from behind a door
that opens to the sea.

I saw the tear in the eyes of an alley
when danger was near.
We had to preserve our tranquility
in all of this ugliness
the beauty of the world is in your name
all doors open four ways:
Wind
Earth
Fire
Water
You have come the right way!
Now cover your trail!

FOR KAVEH

Turn off the lights
close your eyes
and listen to my voice from behind a world,
whose shoulder-snakes have coiled up in the sea.
Today's greatness is in your eyes
fend off their sneers and howls
welcome the water's revolt
and cover up
your steel-blue leather miracle.

FOR AUNT ZAHRA, UNCLE BAKHSHI, UNCLE MAHMOUD, AND AUNT LEILA

Turn out the lights
close your eyes
and listen to my voice from some unknown faraway place.
My father's steady voice and mother's loving calm
are enough for me.
Kelijā could no longer be a safe island
every day
the rocky cliffs grew harder and
the seaside roads grew narrower.
Despite all this
we shouldered the swollen clusters of grapes
pushed back the stony blisters on the graves.

I kiss your glances.
Hide your eyes from the sky's twinkle
and put a veil over the memories of that island.

I MAKE WISHES

Snow doesn't know the fire
that burns the throat
I make wishes:
for Father   a library
for Mother   a house with no kitchen
for myself   a darkroom
for hidden words to appear
for our appearance, all together.

I keep opening and closing my eyes
laughing at sleeping and at being awake
at locks, at walls, at closed doors.

I make wishes:
for my brothers and sister
a key to the waters of the world
for the port, a shore with a loose earring
for the shore, a sea with whirlpools
for the sea, plenty of ships.

The bitter taste of crude oil
travels up the throat
and the two seas part
the dog sniffs the water
fire erupts from the soil
spilling wind on our mouths.

This time
put a mole under my lip
so that the earth doesn't recognize me.
It was a mistake:
I was about to remove my foot from your shoe
but I stepped on a landmine.
Between all of these wishes and this middle east
a flag trembles on a tail
and with each bark
we slip greedily into the skin of a cat
the end.